MAKING SCIENCE WORK

Forces
and
Machines

TERRY JENNINGS

Illustrations by
Peter Smith and
Catherine Ward

RSVP
**RAINTREE
STECK-VAUGHN**
P U B L I S H E R S
The Steck-Vaughn Company

Austin, Texas

1667 6171

Published by Raintree Steck-Vaughn Publishers, an imprint of Steck-Vaughn Company

A Mirabel Book

Produced by Cynthia Parzych Publishing, Inc.
648 Broadway, New York, NY 10012

Designed by Arcadia Consultants

Printed and bound in Spain by International Graphic Service

1   2   3   4   5   6   7   8   9   0   pl   99   98   97   96   95

Library of Congress Cataloging-in-Publication Data
Jennings, Terry J.
    Forces and machines / Terry Jennings ; illustrations by Peter Smith and Catherine Ward.
        p.   cm. — (Making science work)
    Includes index.
    ISBN 0-8172-3961-8
    ISBN 0-8172-4254-6 (softcover)
    1. Machinery—Juvenile literature.   2. Force and energy—Juvenile literature.   [1. Force and energy.   2. Force and energy—Experiments.   3. Simple machines.   4. Simple machines—Experiments.   5. Experiments.]   I. Smith, Peter, 1948- ill.   II. Ward, Catherine, ill.   III. Title.   IV. Series: Jennings, Terry J.   Making science work.
    TJ147.J46   1996
    621.8—dc20   95–11528
                                                                                    CIP
                                                                                    AC

PHOTO CREDITS
Art Directors Photo Library: 8
Belitha Press Ltd.: 6, 21
Benetton Formula Limited: 18
Brookes & Vernons: 24
BSP International Foundations Ltd./Plant Hire Executive: 10
© Robert Frerck, Tony Stone Worldwide, Ltd.: 25
Grove Europe/Plant Hire Executive: 28
Jennings, Dr. Terry: 15
Liebherr-Werk Ehingen Gmbh: 26
Motor Industry Research Association: 19
NASA: 12
Science Photo Library: 13
VME Construction Equipment GB Ltd., photo by Grahame
    Miller: 11

Key to Symbols

 "See for Yourself" element

 Demonstrates the principles of the subject

 Warning! Adult help is required

 Activity for the child to try

Contents

What Is Force?

Forces are all around us. We call any kind of push or pull a force. A force can make things go. A force can stop things. Forces can stretch, bend, and turn things. Some forces are very large. Some are very small. How many times have you used forces today?

A small pushing force

A large pushing force

A twisting force

Pushing and pulling forces

A large pulling force

What Is a Machine?

A machine helps to make work easier. A hammer is a simple machine. With a hammer we can easily knock nails in wood.

A hammer is a simple machine.

A bulldozer is a large machine. A bulldozer makes it easier to move earth and rocks. It uses a lot of force. The big blade at the front pushes earth and rocks out of the way. The blade can move up and down. It can also tip forward and backward.

A bulldozer

There are many other large machines. They all work by making big forces. There are machines that can push and pull. There are machines that lift and turn. Some of these machines are described in this book.

Exhaust

Diesel engine

Controls

Crawler track

Wheel

Blade

What happens when you throw a ball up into the air? The ball comes down. This happens because the Earth pulls things back to the ground. We call this force gravity. Gravity pulls on you and keeps you on the ground. All objects, heavy or light, are pulled down to Earth at the same speed by gravity.

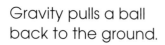

Gravity pulls a ball back to the ground.

When there is no gravity, objects or people float like these astronauts.

8

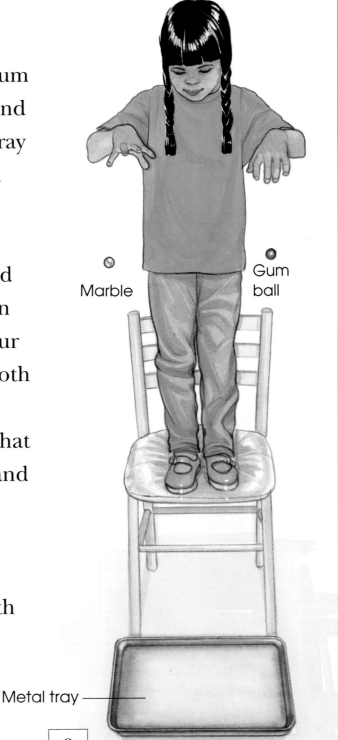

Get a marble, a gum ball, a metal tray, and a chair. Place the tray on the floor. Stand on the chair above the tray. Hold the marble in one hand and the gum ball in the other. Hold your arms high. Drop both things at the same time. You will see that the heavy marble and the light gum ball land at the same time. Gravity pulls them down to Earth at the same speed.

Marble

Gum ball

Metal tray

9

A pile driver

Gravity can be used to do heavy jobs. A pile driver lifts and drops a large weight. The weight falls because of gravity. It hits the steel posts and knocks them into the ground.

A weight on a string always hangs straight down. Gravity pulls the weight down. The string and weight can be used to check that things are standing up perfectly straight. This is called a plumb line. Builders use a plumb line to check that walls are straight.

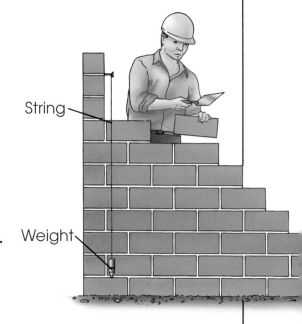

String

Weight

Using a plumb line

10

Gravity can also help a hammer to knock a nail into wood. Gravity makes water move down a hill. Gravity makes the earth pour out of a truck. Dump trucks can drop their loads because of gravity.

Gravity helps a dump truck to drop its load.

Rockets

The Earth's gravity is very strong. Spacecraft have to make a force bigger than the Earth's gravity to travel into space. The space shuttle needs huge rocket engines to push it into the air. Inside the rocket engines, fuel is burned very quickly. Hot gases shoot from the rocket. They push the rocket into space.

The space shuttle *Atlantis* being launched

The moon is smaller than the Earth. Its force of gravity is not as strong as that of the Earth. On the moon, an astronaut weighs much less than he or she weighs on Earth.

Flight deck

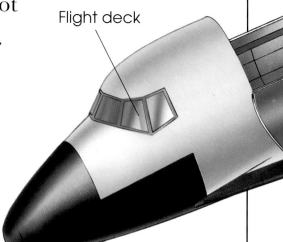

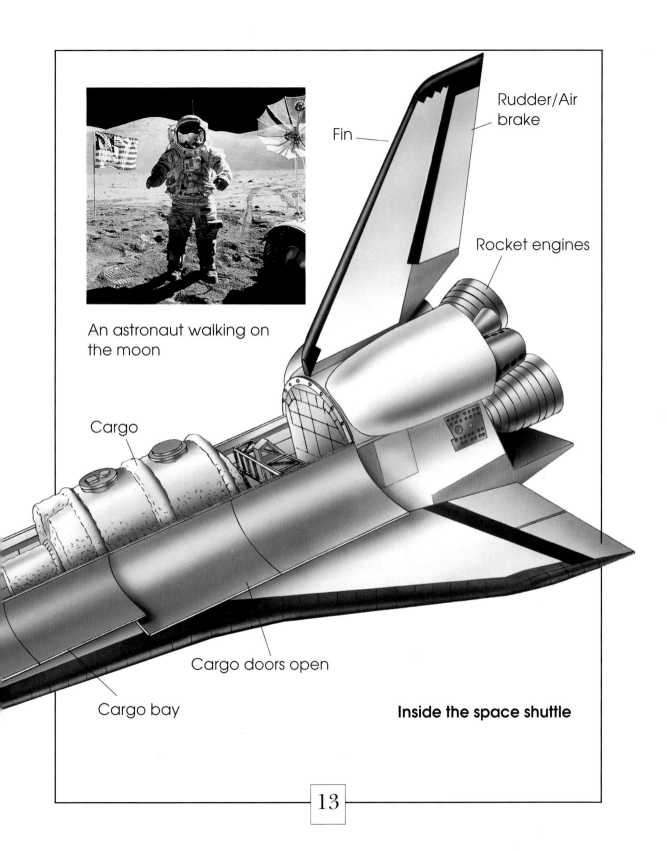

An astronaut walking on the moon

Fin

Rudder/Air brake

Rocket engines

Cargo

Cargo doors open

Cargo bay

Inside the space shuttle

The Force of Friction

When you pedal a bicycle, the back wheel turns. This pushes the bike forward. If you stop pedaling on a flat surface, the bike slows down. The wheels slow down because they rub against the road. This rubbing makes a force called friction. Friction makes things slow down and stop.

A bumpy surface makes more friction than a smooth one. You can slide on ice because there is hardly any friction. It is not easy to walk or run on ice. Friction helps you to hold on to a surface.

Machines have moving parts that rub against each other. This friction slows the machine down and makes the parts wear out. When oil is put on the moving parts, it makes them slide more easily.

Oiling a bicycle

The forces used in riding a bicycle

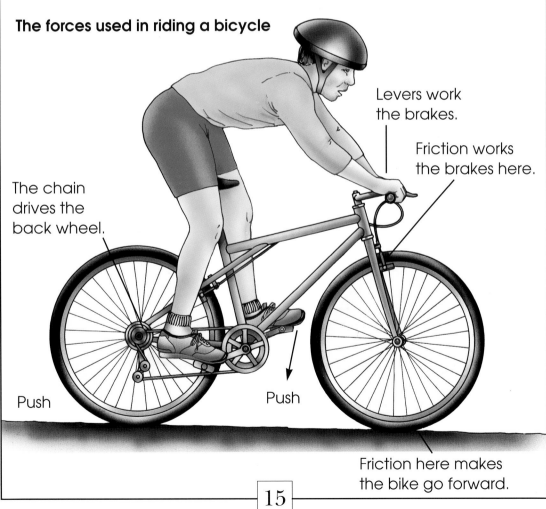

Levers work
the brakes.

Friction works
the brakes here.

The chain
drives the
back wheel.

Push

Push

Friction here makes
the bike go forward.

Get an eraser, a stone, a small piece of wood, and an ice cube. Put these things in a line on a smooth wooden board, about 3 feet (1 m) long. Carefully place a book under the end of the wooden board. Which things slide down the board? Now put them back at the end of the wooden board. Place two books under the board. Which things move this time? Do they move more easily? Do they move less easily? Cover the wooden board with cloth. Repeat the experiment. Which surface has more friction?

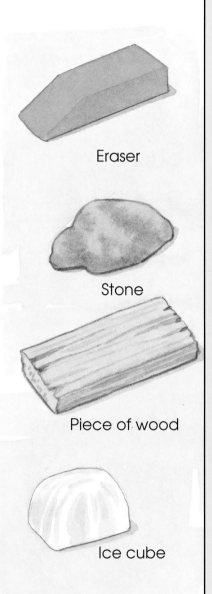

Eraser

Stone

Piece of wood

Ice cube

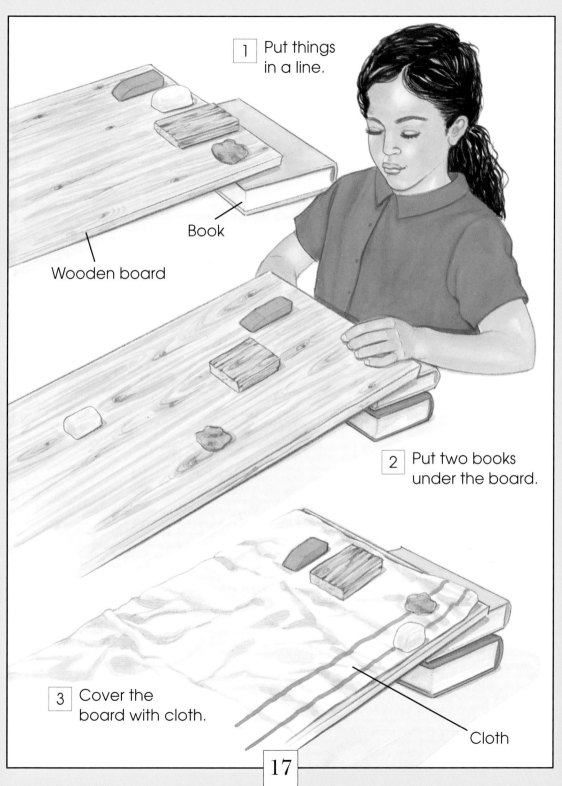

1 Put things in a line.

Book

Wooden board

2 Put two books under the board.

3 Cover the board with cloth.

Cloth

17

The faster you go, the more air you have to push through. Friction slows you down. Airplanes and fast cars are shaped so that the air moves past them easily. This causes less friction. Shaping something to cause less friction is called streamlining.

A racing car is streamlined. It is shaped so that the air flows over it easily. There are no large flat surfaces that stick up and push against the air.

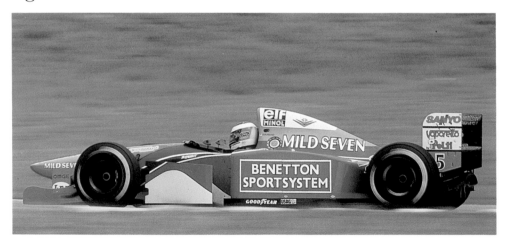

A racing car is streamlined to cause less friction.

Engineers use a wind tunnel to test car shapes. This tells them if the cars are streamlined. Powerful fans make air move past the car. Engineers can see which parts of the car stop the air. Streamlined cars and airplanes can go faster. They also use less fuel.

Testing a car in a wind tunnel

Levers are simple machines. Simple machines make it easier to do work. Levers can change a small force into a large one. Levers can also change the direction of a force. All levers move things. The thing you want to move is called the load. The work of lifting, pulling, or turning is called the effort. The place where the lever turns is called the fulcrum.

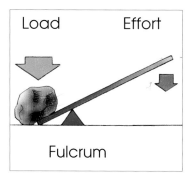

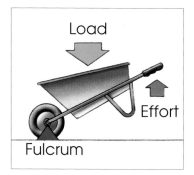

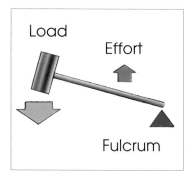

There are three main types of levers.

There are hundreds of different kinds of levers. Many of the things you use every day are levers. You can use the handle of a spoon to lift a lid. The spoon is used as a lever. A pump handle, a door, and a hammer are also levers.

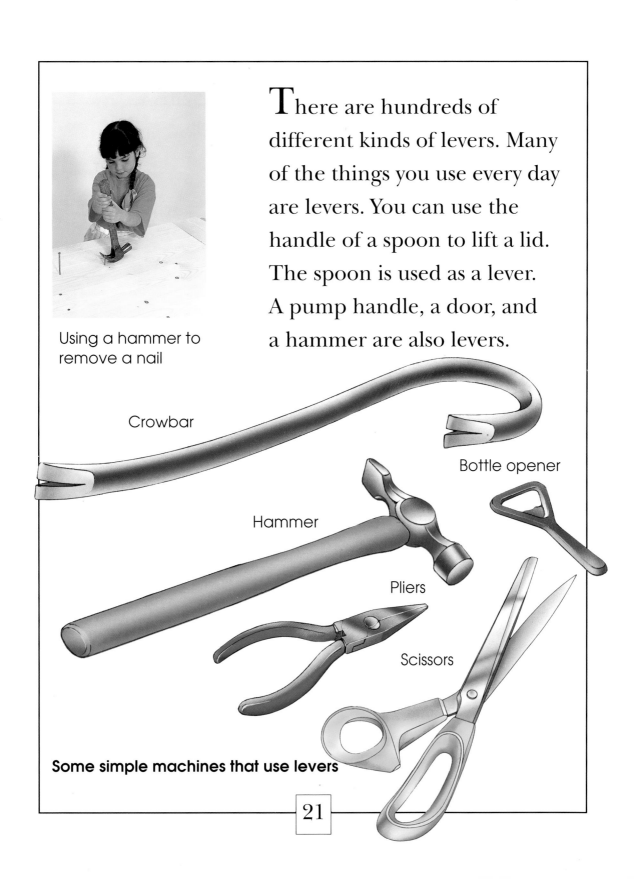

Using a hammer to remove a nail

Crowbar

Bottle opener

Hammer

Pliers

Scissors

Some simple machines that use levers

Make a lever. Balance a 12-inch (31-cm) ruler across a pencil to do this. Rest a heavy book (the load) on the first inch (3 cm) of the ruler. Slide the pencil (the fulcrum) under the 8-inch (21-cm) mark of the ruler. Use one finger to press down on the end of the ruler (the effort).

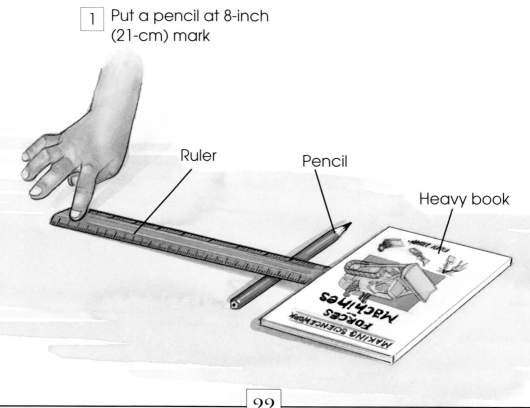

1   Put a pencil at 8-inch (21-cm) mark

Ruler

Pencil

Heavy book

MAKING SCIENCE WORK
FORCES and
Machines

Now move the pencil to the 4-inch (11-cm) mark on the ruler. Press down on the end of the ruler with the same finger. Is it easier or harder to raise the book now? Levers lift things most easily when the fulcrum is as close to the load end as possible.

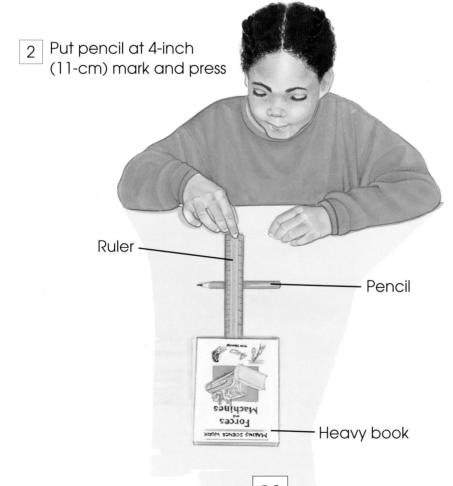

2 | Put pencil at 4-inch (11-cm) mark and press

Ruler

Pencil

Heavy book

Backhoes and Fire Engines

Many large machines use levers. Backhoes are machines that dig holes. The digger is made in two parts. These are called the boom and the arm. The boom, the arm, and the bucket are all levers.

A backhoe being used to dig a hole.

The platform of a fire engine works like a backhoe. The boom is made in two parts. Each of these parts is a lever. The platform on which the fire fighters stand is also a lever. This platform can lift fire fighters high above the ground. They can then fight fires and rescue people from tall buildings.

The platform on which the fire fighters stand is a lever.

Like levers, pulleys also make it easier to lift things. A pulley is a grooved wheel with a rope, a chain, or a cable over it. The end is tied to something heavy. One pulley does not change the effort needed to do a job. But it is easier to pull a rope down than it is to lift something heavy up. Two pulleys make it even easier to lift something heavy. But you have to pull the rope twice as far.

Pulleys make it easier to lift heavy objects.

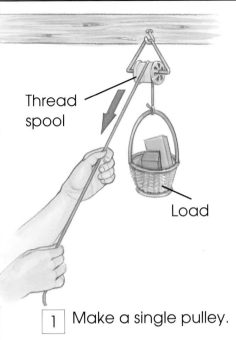

Thread spool

Load

1 Make a single pulley.

Make your own pulley. Push some stiff wire through a thread spool. Bend the ends of the wire into a triangle. Hang the pulley from a hook. Tie one end of some string to a weight. Put the string over the pulley. Measure how far you have to pull the string to lift the weight one foot (31 cm).

Thread spools

Load

2 Make a double pulley.

Now use two pulleys. You need four thread spools. Use the same weight you used before. How far do you have to pull the string to lift the weight one foot (31 cm)?

Cranes and Elevators

Cranes use pulleys to lift and move heavy loads. This tower crane is used for work on tall buildings. The hook of the crane hangs from a load block on a trolley. The counterweight is made of heavy concrete blocks. The counterweight stops the load from pulling the crane over.

This crane can be moved. The hook hangs from a load block. The counterweight is built into the bottom of the crane. Folding feet keep the crane from falling over.

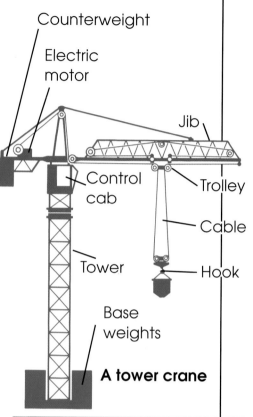

Counterweight

Electric motor

Jib

Trolley

Control cab

Cable

Tower

Hook

Base weights

A tower crane

A mobile crane

An elevator has a heavy counterweight. This balances the weight of the car. The elevator motor, then, only has to lift the weight of people and goods inside the elevator car.

Pulley

Motor

Car

Counterweight

1 2 3 4 5

An elevator

Push a knitting needle through a thread spool. Lay a heavy book on the needle. Put a piece of thin string over the thread spool. Tie a plastic cup of sand on the end of the string. This is your counterweight. Tie a small box to the other end of the string. This is your elevator car. Put modeling clay in the box. Does your elevator move down? Take some of the clay out of the box. Does the elevator go up?

Heavy book

Knitting needle

Thread spool

String

Plastic cup of sand

Clay

Small box

Glossary

Backhoe A large digging machine in which the bucket is at the end of a hinged arm.

Balance To keep or make something steady; to share weight equally on both sides of something.

Blade The wide, flat part of something such as a shovel or a bulldozer.

Cable A strong rope or wire.

Concrete A material made of cement, sand, and water.

Counterweight A weight used to balance something heavy, so that it can be moved easily.

Crane A large machine with a long arm. The arm can move up and down and left and right. Cranes are used to lift and carry heavy objects.

Effort The force needed to do work.

Force Any kind of pushing or pulling.

Friction The force that slows down moving objects; the drag when two surfaces are rubbed together.

Fuel Anything that is burned to make heat energy such as coal, gas, oil, or wood.

Fulcrum The point at which a lever turns.

Gravity The force that attracts things toward the Earth.

Lever A simple machine with a bar that turns around a fixed point. Levers are used for lifting weights or forcing something open.

Load The weight moved by a simple machine.

Pile driver A machine for driving down piles, or poles, into the ground.

Pulley A simple machine that has a wheel with a groove in the rim for a rope to run over. It is used to lift things.

Simple machine A machine that has few or no moving parts.

Streamlining Making something, such as an airplane, car, or ship, so that it moves smoothly through the air or water.

Index